R. TYLER GATCHELL JR. PETER NEUFELD ·PATRICK
IN ASSOCIATION WITH THE McCARTER THEATRE PRESENT

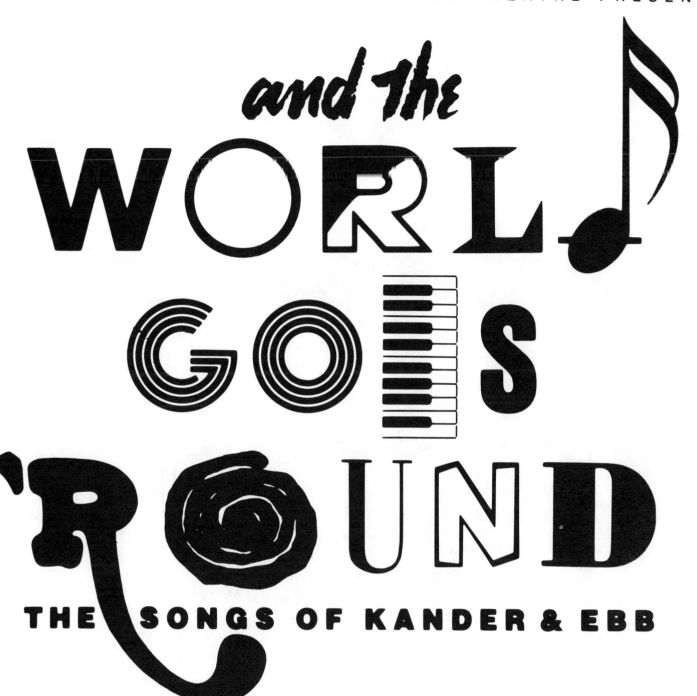

MUSIC BY JOHN KANDER LYRICS BY FRED EBB
CONCEIVED BY SCOTT ELLIS SUSAN STROMAN DAVID THOMPSON

JOHN KANDER

Photo by BERIL TOWBIN

JOHN KANDER and FRED EBB
(Composer and Lyricist)

For the Theatre: *Flora, The Red Menace; Cabaret; The Happy Time; Zorba; 70 Girls 70; Chicago; The Act; Woman of the Year; The Rink; Kiss of the Spider Woman.* For Films: *Cabaret; Norman Rockwell: A Short Subject; Lucky Lady; New York, New York; Funny Lady; A Matter of Time; French Postcards; Stepping Out;* and the upcoming *Billy Bathgate.* For Television: *Liza* (Liza Minnelli); *Gypsy In My Soul* (Shirley MacLaine); *Goldie and Liza Together* (Goldie Hawn and Liza Minnelli); *Ol' Blue Eyes Is Back* (Frank Sinatra); *Baryshnikov On Broadway; An Early Frost; Liza In London.* In Concert: Joel Grey; Chita Rivera; Ann Margaret; Carol Channing; and the recent *Stepping Out with Liza Minnelli* at Radio City Music Hall.

FRED EBB

Photo by SHELDON RAMSTELL

CONTENTS

Selections Prepared By PAUL McKIBBINS

BUT THE WORLD GOES 'ROUND

Lyrics by FRED EBB
Music by JOHN KANDER

5

6

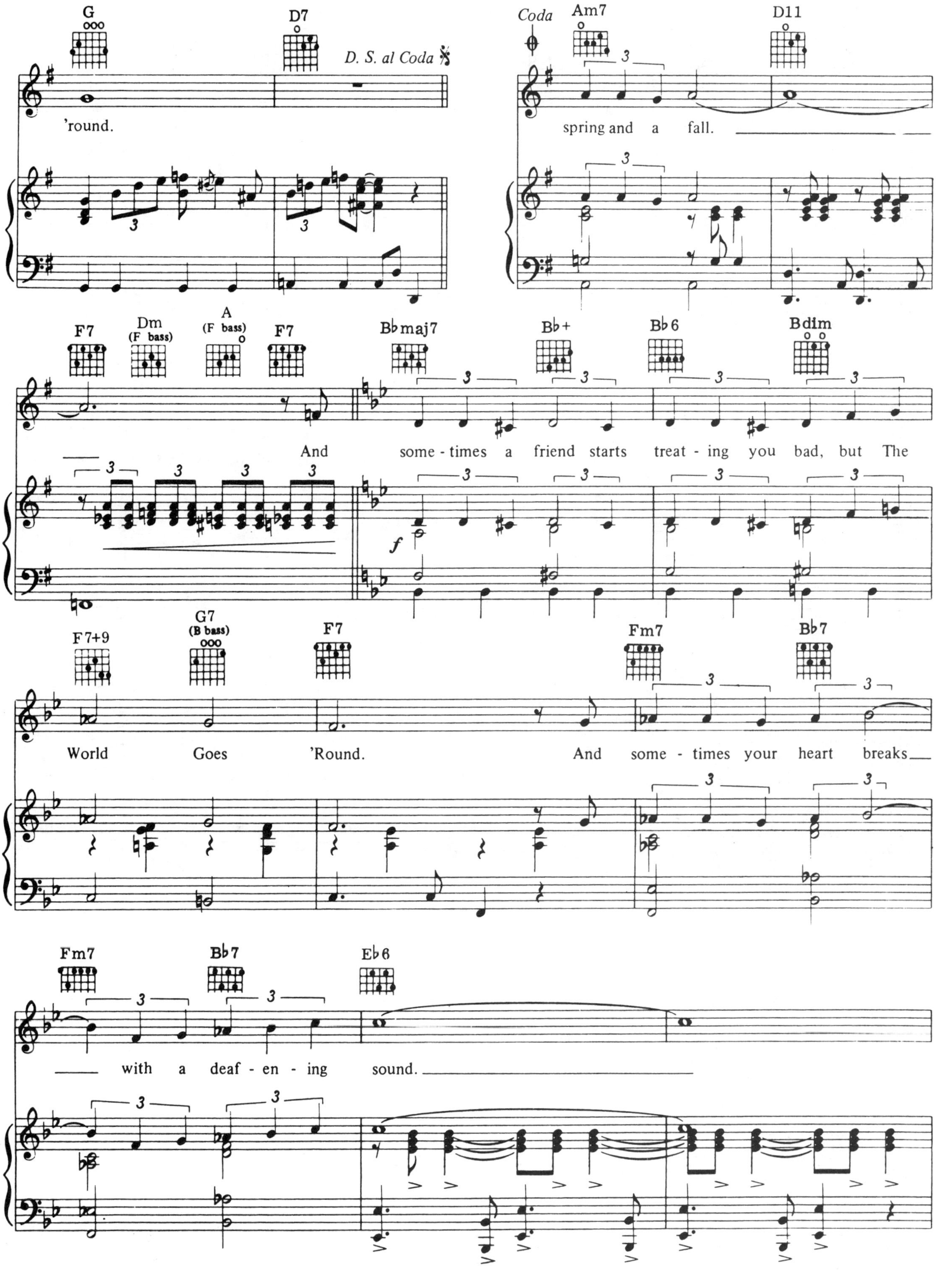

'round.

D. S. al Coda 𝄋

Coda

spring and a fall. _____ _____

And _____ some-times a friend starts treat-ing you bad, but The

World Goes 'Round. And some-times your heart breaks____

_____ with a deaf-en-ing sound. _____

YES

Lyrics by FRED EBB
Music by JOHN KANDER

Moderato (with a lilt)

Yes. Say "Yes."

Life keeps hap-pen-ing ev-'ry day. Say "Yes." When

pos - si - bil - i-ties come your way, you can't start won-der-ing what to say. You
mink and mar - i-gold right out - side and long white Cad-il-lacs you can ride. But

COFFEE (In A Cardboard Cup)

Lyrics by FRED EBB
Music by JOHN KANDER

THE HAPPY TIME

Lyrics by FRED EBB
Music by JOHN KANDER

COLORED LIGHTS

Lyrics by FRED EBB
Music by JOHN KANDER

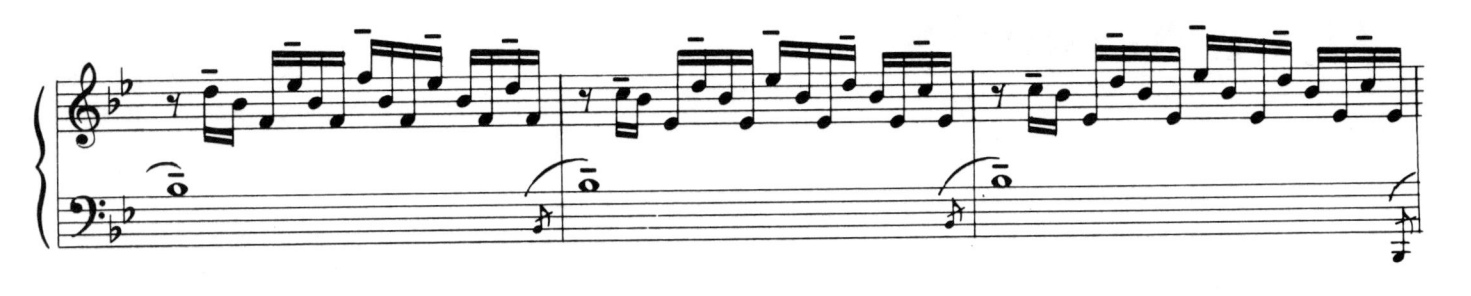

I was

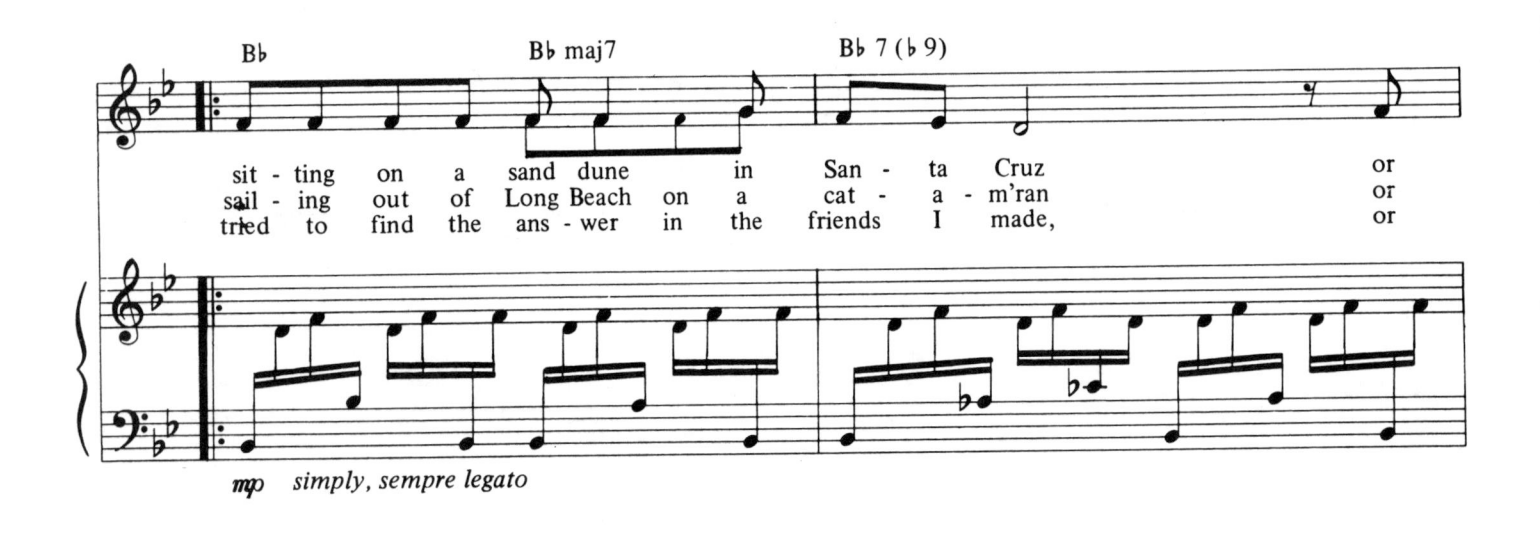

sit - ting on a sand dune in San - ta Cruz or
sail - ing out of Long Beach on a cat - a - m'ran or
tried to find the ans - wer in the friends I made, or

mp simply, sempre legato

Mon - ter - ey. Well, an - y - way, I could
fish - ing scow. Well, an - y - how, I was
beds I'd share, well, an - y - where. But with

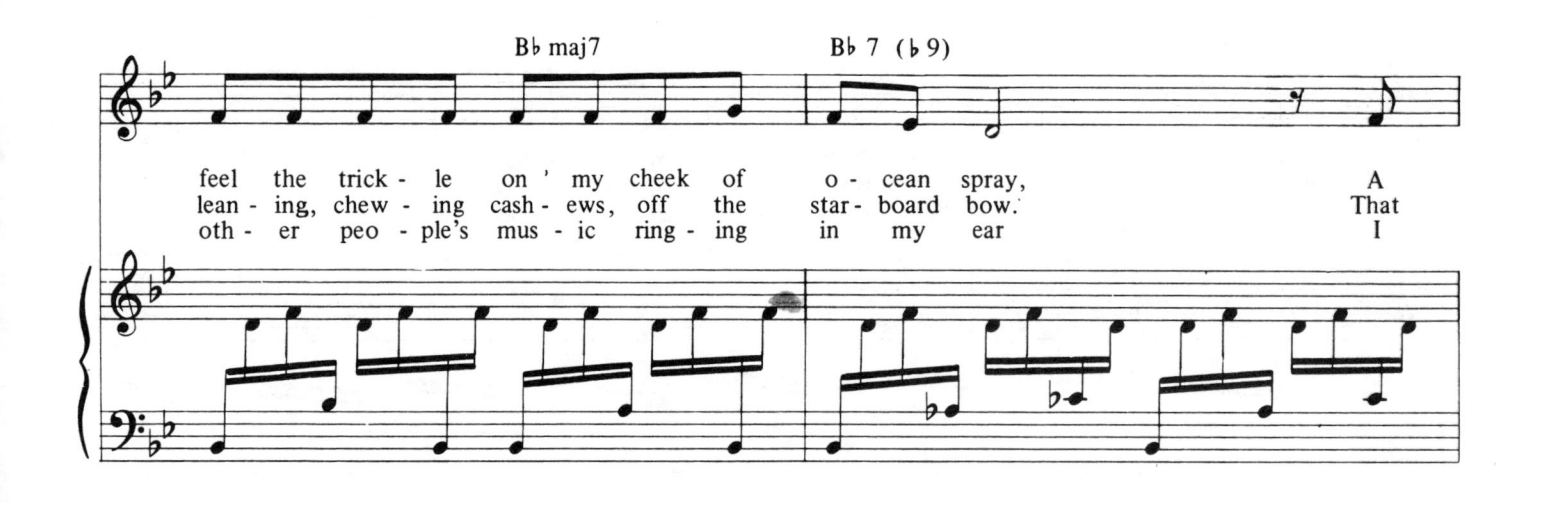

Fred? ... Well, an - y - way, I
Pete? ... Well, an - y - how, I
ten? ... Well, an - y - way, it

should be up and yet I'm down in - stead. Some - thing's
won - der why I feel so in - com - plete. Some - thing's
seems to me I knew the se - cret then. It's so

miss - ing, Sam;___ some - thing's miss - ing, Fred. ___ Some - thing's
miss - ing, Joe;___ some - thing's miss - ing, Pete. ___ Some - thing's
sim - ple: twelve.___ It's so sim - ple: ten. ___ It was

thump - ing oom - pah - pah or - gan sound.

Nois - y boys, long and lean.

Gig - gles of girls in the mez - za - nine.

Fil - tered through Col - ored Lights,

Gold and am - ber and green.

I was
And I

Pass - ing smiles 'round and 'round thump - ing

oom - pah - pah or - gan sound.

Nois - y boys, long and lean, Gig - gles of

girls in the mez - za - nine.

Leav - ing home years a - go

what was I look-ing for? I don't know.

I can't re - call well, an - y way.

SARA LEE

Lyrics by FRED EBB
Music by JOHN KANDER

Hil - ton. He ca - ters ban - quets and at each af - fair, He'll

I really know what you mean.
(sim.) *Aren't her brownies obscene?*

swear by Sa - ra Lee, Sa - ra Lee, Drop that

cresc. e rall.

"H," Say "Sa - ra, Sa - ra Lee." And that's o - kay by me.

cresc. e rall.

Broad cakewalk

I love her cheese - cake white as pearl.

ARTHUR

Lyrics by FRED EBB
Music by JOHN KANDER

Latin

He has a small a-part-ment in the cen-ter of town.___ I'd

hard-ly say___ it was posh. But I gun my Grem-lin and I

hur-ry on down___ To hear the ban-nis-ter squeak. And the wa-ter-bed slush. So,

Rock

you can have your T. M.___ Ev-'ry A. M., ev-'ry P. M.___ But

don't sit there and glow-er,___ Just pick an-oth-er ho-ur___ For your round trip tick - et

moon. You got - ta try Ar - thur,_ I re - com-mend Ar - thur._

He's list - ed as Ar - thur,_ in the af - ter-noon.__

MY COLORING BOOK

Lyrics by FRED EBB
Music by JOHN KANDER

I DON'T REMEMBER YOU

Lyrics by FRED EBB
Music by JOHN KANDER

I DON'T RE - MEM-BER YOU. I DON'T RE - MEM-BER YOU.

I don't re - call a sin - gle thing we used to say or do.

What danc - ing in the park? What laugh - ter in the dark?
(Girl's Lyric): What pic - nic by the mill? What race a - cross the hill?

SOMETIMES A DAY GOES BY

Lyrics by FRED EBB
Music by JOHN KANDER

AND ALL THAT JAZZ

Lyrics by FRED EBB
Music by JOHN KANDER

58

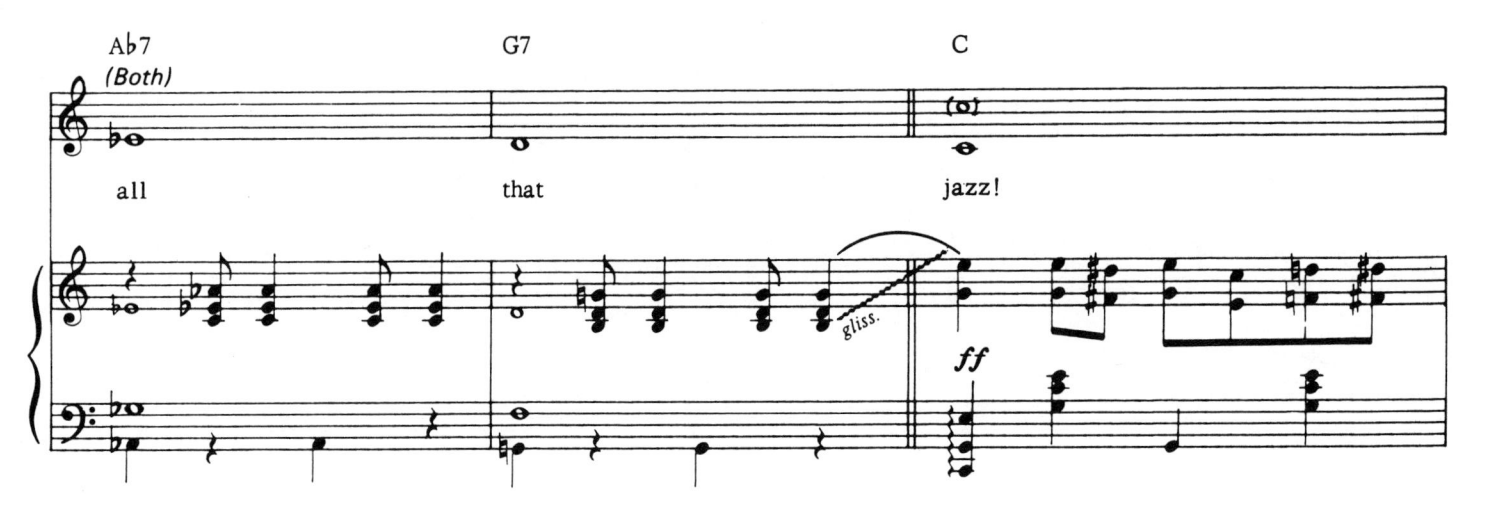

all　　　　　that　　　　　jazz!

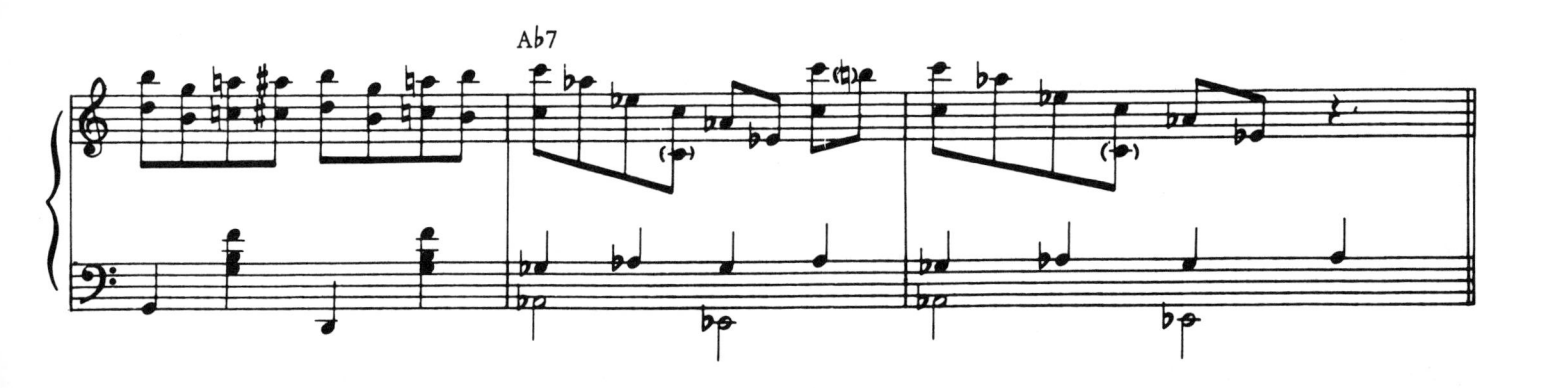

CLASS

Lyrics by FRED EBB
Music by JOHN KANDER

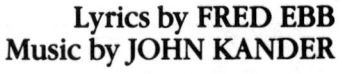

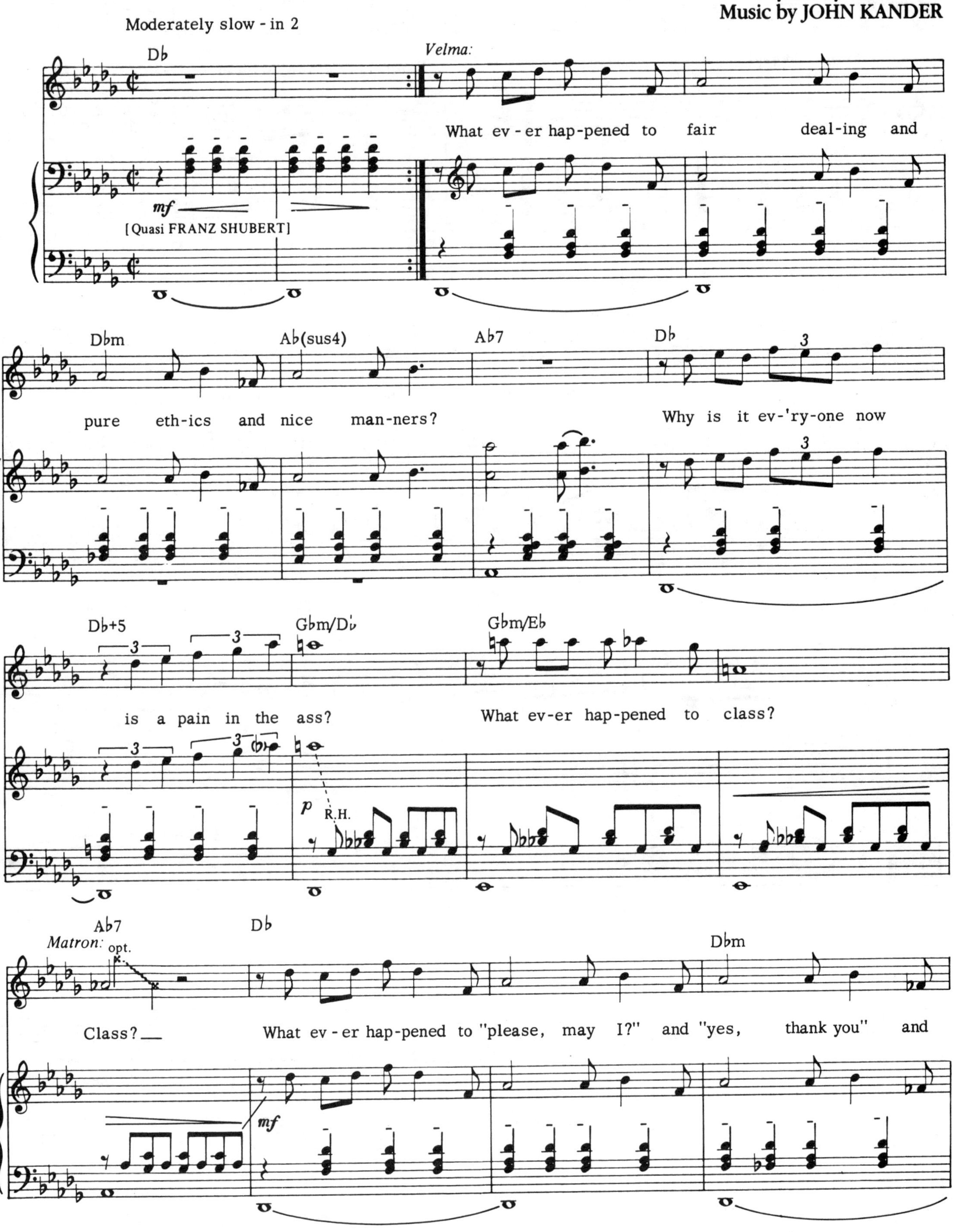
Moderately slow - in 2
Db
Velma:
What ev - er hap-pened to fair deal-ing and
mf
[Quasi FRANZ SHUBERT]
Dbm
Ab(sus4)
Ab7
Db
pure eth-ics and nice man-ners? Why is it ev-'ry-one now
3
Db+5
Gbm/Db
Gbm/Eb
is a pain in the ass? What ev-er hap-pened to class?
p
R.H.
Ab7
Db
Dbm
Matron: opt.
Class? What ev - er hap-pened to "please, may I?" and "yes, thank you" and
mf

MR. CELLOPHANE

Lyrics by FRED EBB
Music by JOHN KANDER

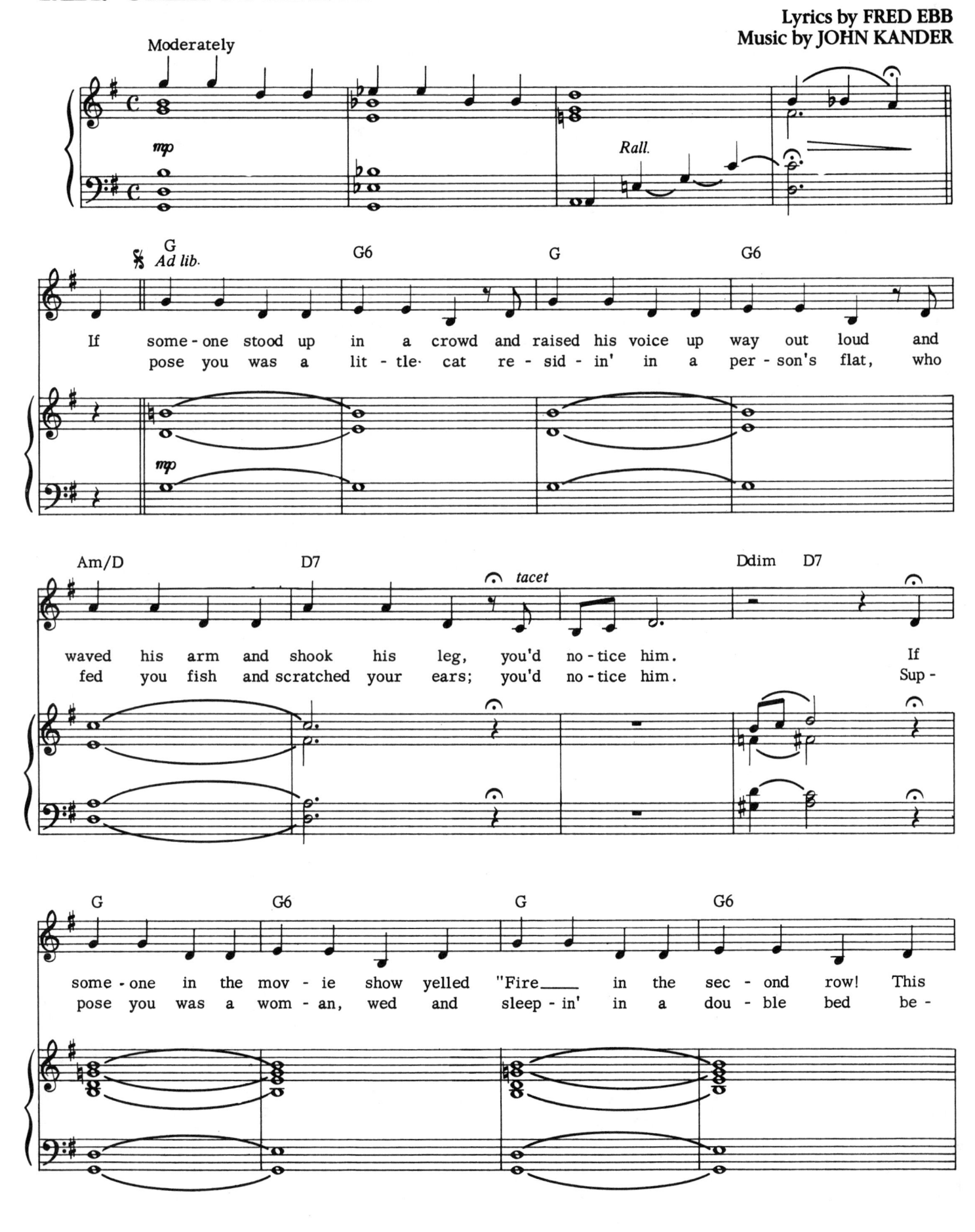

ME AND MY BABY

Lyrics by FRED EBB
Music by JOHN KANDER

1. Me and my ba - by, my ba - by and me, _____ We're 'bout as hap -
2. Look-a my ba - by, my ba - by and me, _____ A dream of a du -
3. Look-a my ba - by, my ba - by and me, _____ Fac - ing the world _____

- py as ba - bies can be. _____ What if I find _____ that I'm
- o, now don't you a - gree? _____ Why keep it mum _____ when there's
- op - ti - mis - ti - cal - ly; _____ Noth - in' can stop _____ us, so

THERE GOES THE BALL GAME

Lyrics by FRED EBB
Music by JOHN KANDER

Moderate tempo (with a beat)

f (finger snap)

There Goes The Ball Game___ 'sall o-ver now,___

There Goes The Ball Game___ I lost and how.___

Came to bat at the be-gin-ning think-ing that my team was win-ning,

8va bassa

HOW LUCKY CAN YOU GET

Lyrics by FRED EBB
Music by JOHN KANDER

80

81

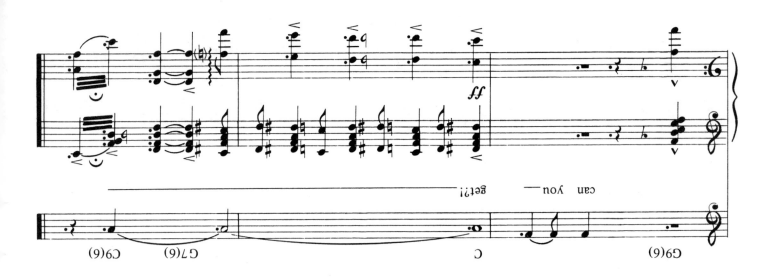

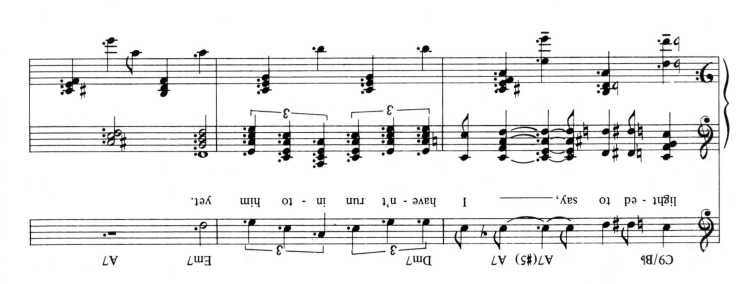

THE RINK

Lyrics by FRED EBB
Music by JOHN KANDER

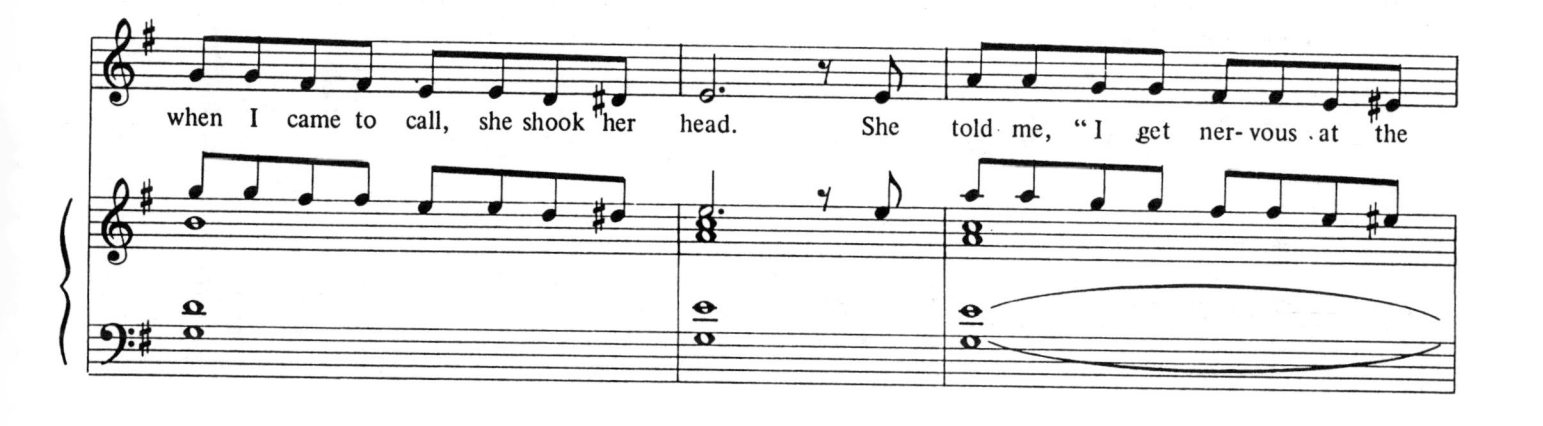

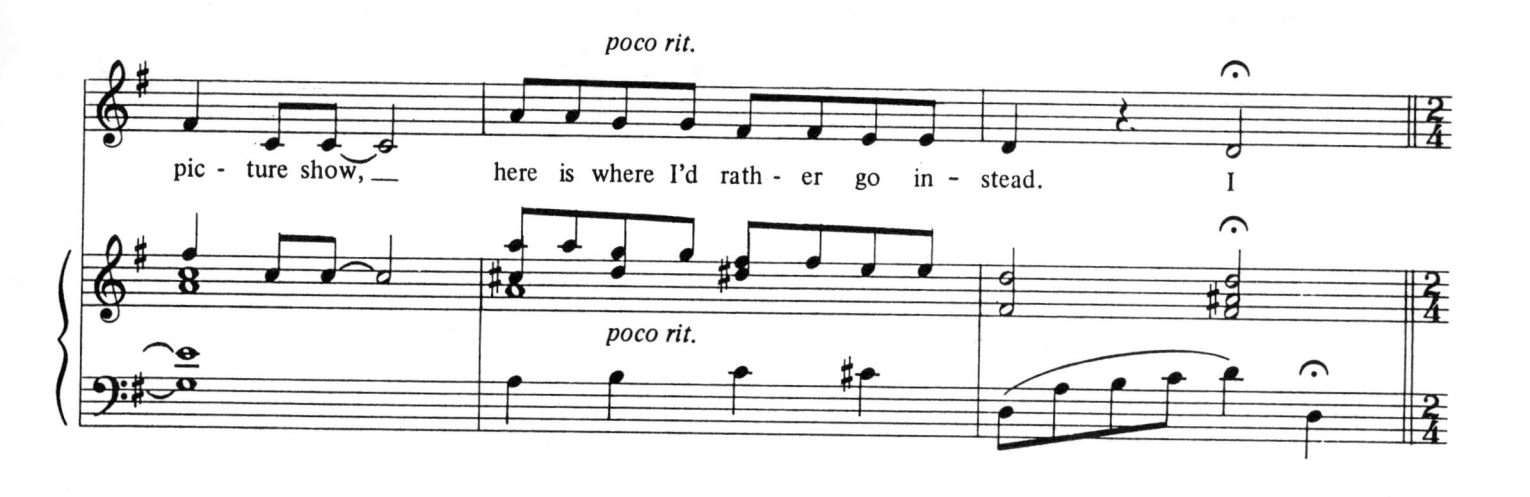

88

68

skate key clink. If you wan - na good go 'round with me, we're gon - na go 'round The
skate key clink. If

Rink!

(1.)

At you wan - na good go

'round with me, if you wan - na gain some ground with me, pure hap - pi - ness can be

Rubato
follow voice

RING THEM BELLS

Lyrics by FRED EBB
Music by JOHN KANDER

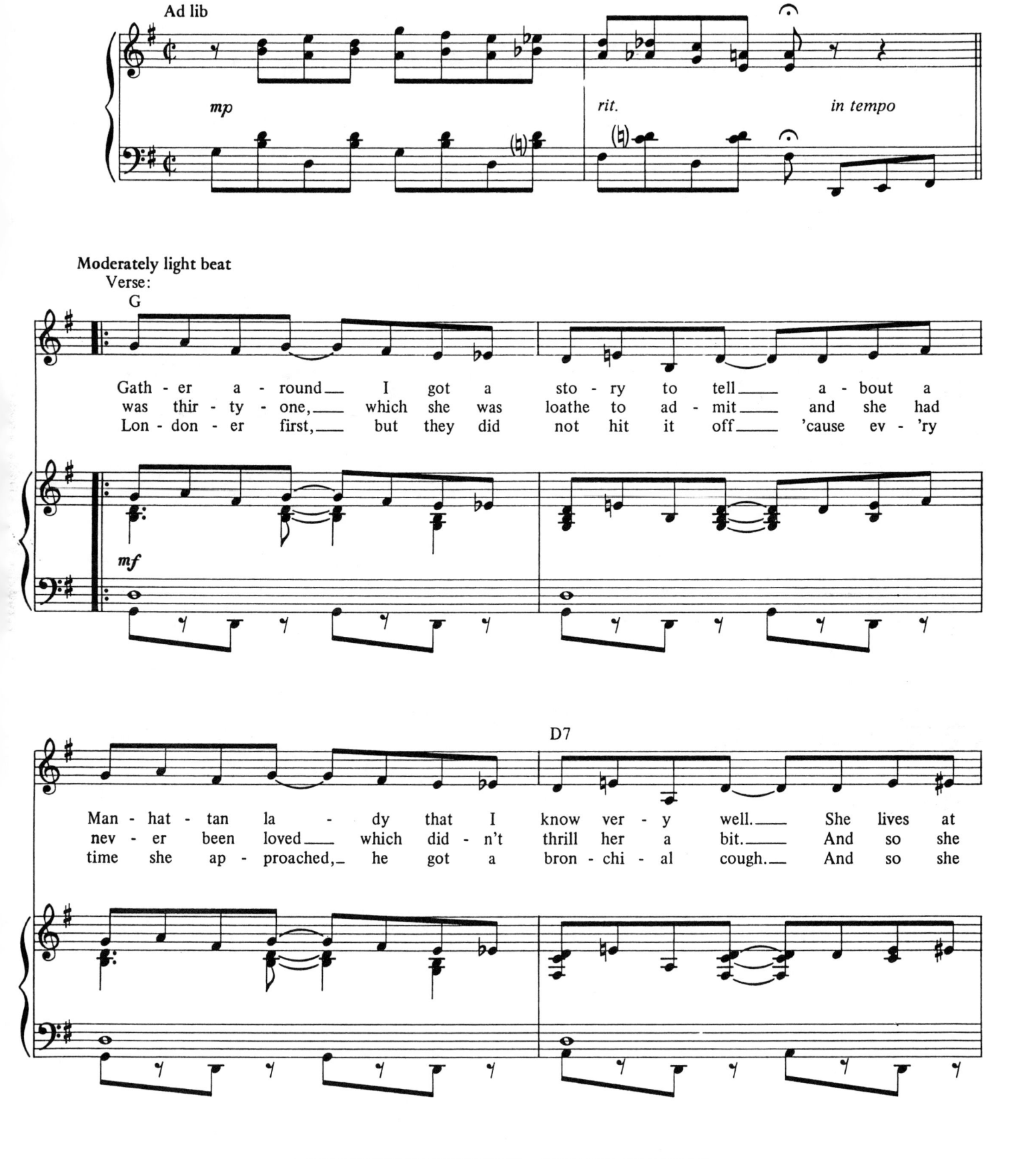

KISS OF THE SPIDER WOMAN

Lyrics by FRED EBB
Music by JOHN KANDER

Soon - er or la - ter you're cer - tain to meet   In the
Soon - er or la - ter your love will ar - rive   And the

ONLY LOVE

Lyrics by FRED EBB
Music by JOHN KANDER

Slowly

Love give me love on-ly love___ What else is there?

Two eyes,___ not see-ing and two arms,___ not shar-ing and

two lips___ not feel-ing. What good are they?

Does-n't the night seem end-less? Does-n't the day go slow?

Does-n't the dark look friend-less and oh,_____ What good is that?

MARRY ME

Lyrics by FRED EBB
Music by JOHN KANDER

A QUIET THING

Lyrics by FRED EBB
Music by JOHN KANDER

Slowly, with feeling

Piano

Chorus *(Lyrically)*

When it all comes true, Just the way you planned, It's fun-ny, but the bells don't ring. It's A QUI-ET THING.

When you hold the world in your trem-bling hand, You'd think you'd hear a

I don't hear the band, The sounds I'm told such mo - ments

bring,_____ Hap - pi - ness comes in on tip - toe._____

Well, what-d'-ya know!_____ It's A QUI-ET THING,_____ A

ver - y QUI - ET THING. THING._____

PAIN

Lyrics by FRED EBB
Music by JOHN KANDER

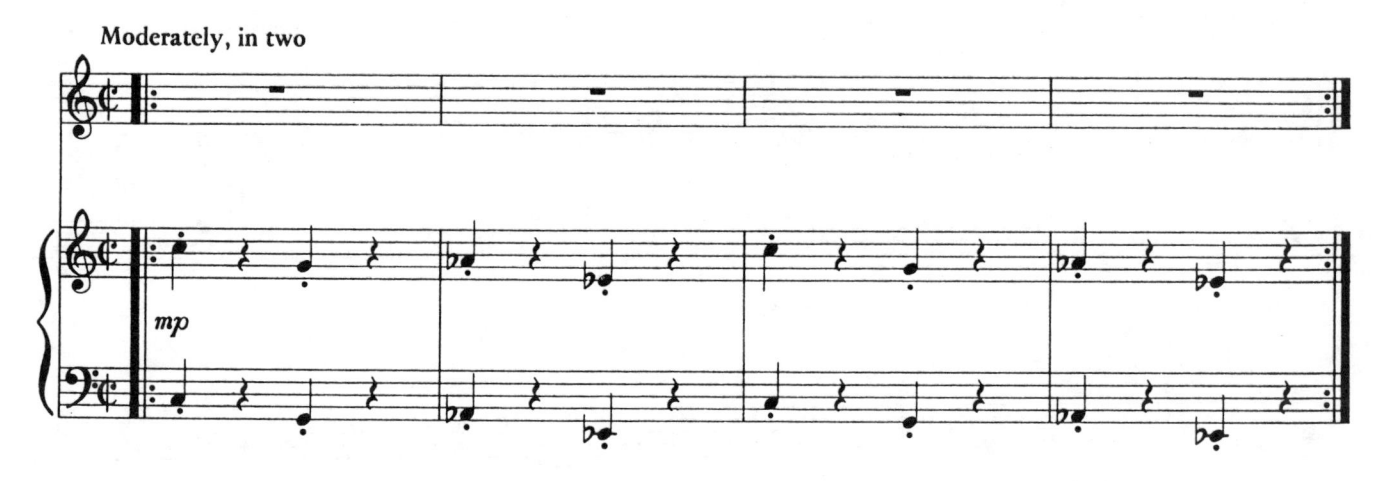

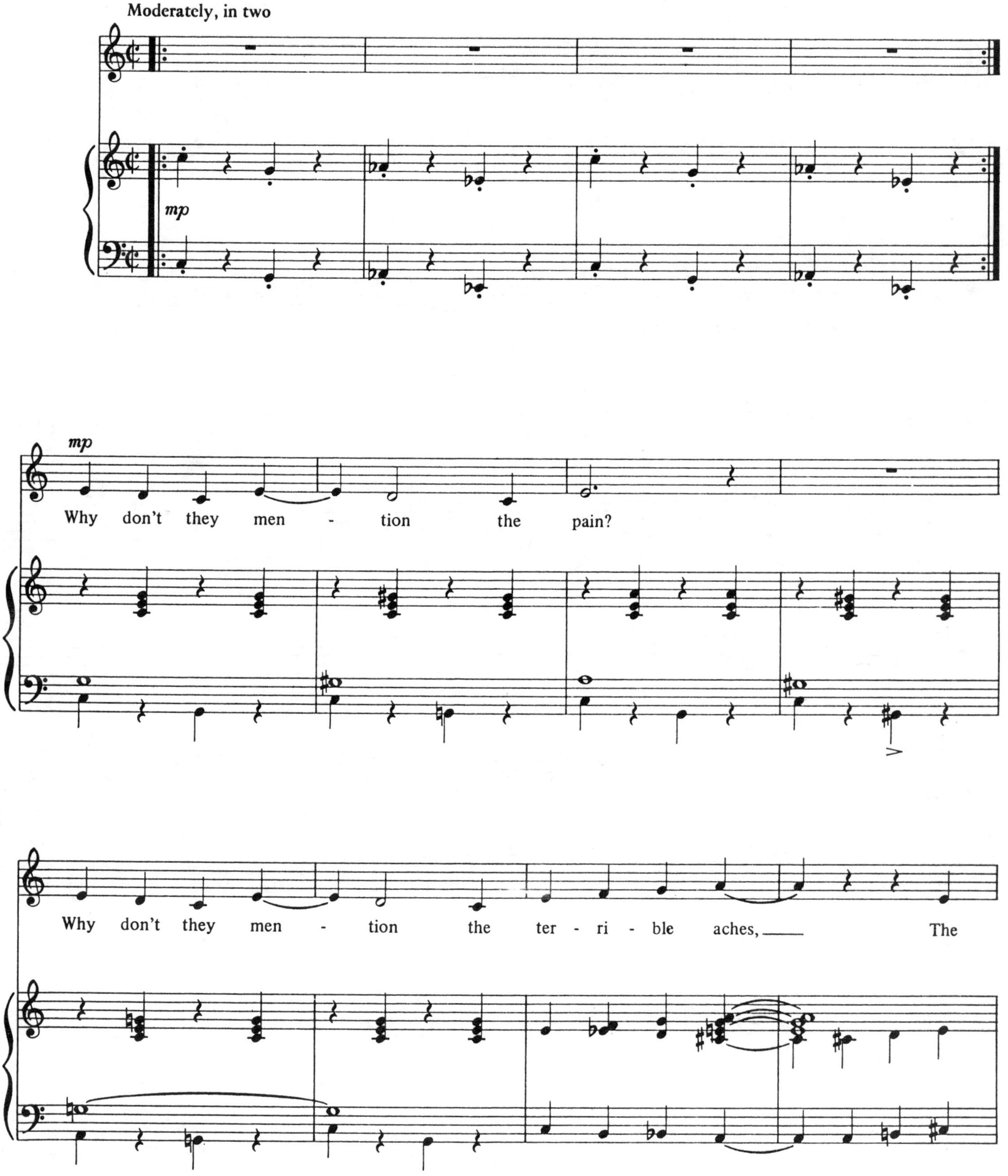
Moderately, in two
mp
mp
Why don't they men - tion the pain?
Why don't they men - tion the ter - ri - ble aches, The

(Spoken:)

I met a friend___ with a cast on his spine.___ I said,

"Oh, in a crash?" He said, "No, *Cho-rus Line*. (Sung:) Can you help me

lo-cate my disk?" Why don't they men - tion the

risk?___ And oh,___

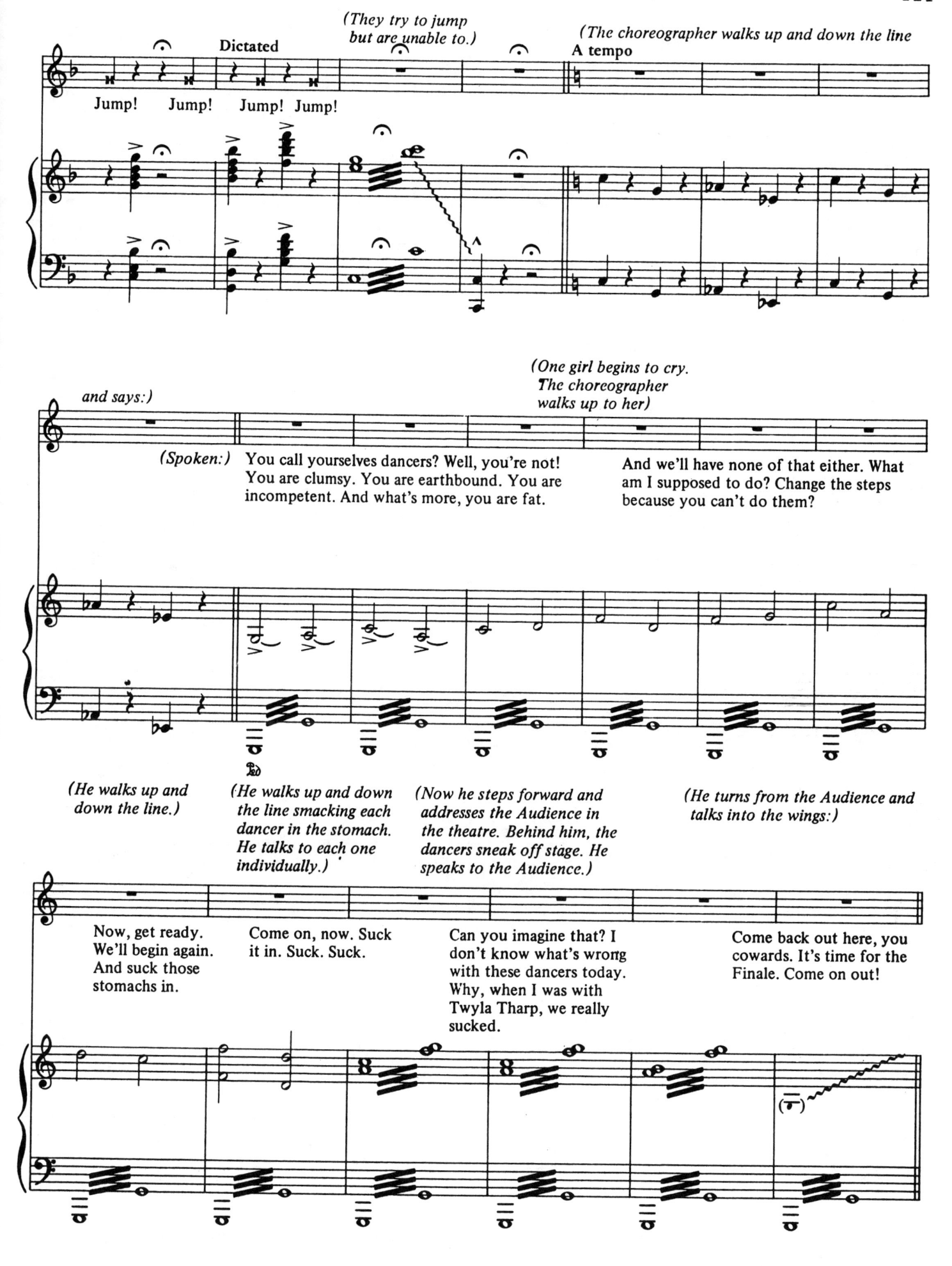

(The dancers reappear on crutches.)

(Sung:)
Why don't they men - tion the scars? Why don't they speak___ of the glis - ten - ing brow___ When they an - nounce I've a her - ni - a now___ When - ev - er I jump I see stars,___ Why don't they men - tion the scars? Oh, they nev - er men - tion the

pain._____ Why do we do____ it? Well, here's the re - ply:___

A danc - er's com - mit - ted, You dance or you die.____ "Com -

mit - ted" im - plies you're in - sane._____ And sure, we got

rocks in the brain._____ But we

THE GRASS IS ALWAYS GREENER

Lyrics by FRED EBB
Music by JOHN KANDER

Dm7 **G7** **C6**

First you brown an on - ion. Is your pic - ture up at Sar - di's?
First you sell the Tup - per - ware.__ The pub - lic wants your aut - o - graph.
That's won - der - ful!

C(6)

What's so won - der - ful? You can clean an ov - en.__
What's so won - der - ful? You raised a teen - aged daugh - ter.__
That's won - der - ful!

A7 **Ddim7** **G7** **Eb** **Ebmaj7**

What's so won - der - ful?
First, you get the "Z - e - off!"
First, you find her di - a - phragm.
Ah _____ The

Ah _____ The

130

132

Ah, think a-bout it, dear - y. The grass is al - ways green - er

Ah, think a-bout it, dear - y. The grass is al - ways green - er

in some - one els - e's yard.

in some - one els - e's yard.

D. S. al Coda

(Spoken:) *It's hard!*

(Spoken:) *It's hard!*

Coda

First, you keep your mouth shut. I bet you squeeze the Char-min. That's won-der-ful!

What's so won-der-ful? You can make a head-line. That's won-der-ful!

What's so won-der-ful? I'd

So go and brown an on-ion. (Spoken:) You've al-read-y had my hus-band!

rath-er have a pot roast. And have some peace and qui-et.

WE CAN MAKE IT

Lyrics by FRED EBB
Music by JOHN KANDER

MAYBE THIS TIME

Lyrics by FRED EBB
Music by JOHN KANDER

F   **Am9(no 7)**   **C**   **A9**   **D7**   **G9**   **C**

an - y - more,_ like the last time_ and   the time be - fore._   Ev - 'ry - bo - dy_

C+5   **C6**   **C9**   **F**

loves a win - ner_   so no - bo - dy_ loved me.   La - dy Peace - ful._

F+5   **Dm7**   **F#°**   **G7**

La - dy Hap - py._   That's what I long to be.   All the odds are_

Am   **D13**   **C/G**

in my fa - vor_   Some - thing's bound to be - gin.   It's got to hap - pen_

ISN'T THIS BETTER?

Lyrics by FRED EBB
Music by JOHN KANDER

Now I am calm, safe and ser - ene.

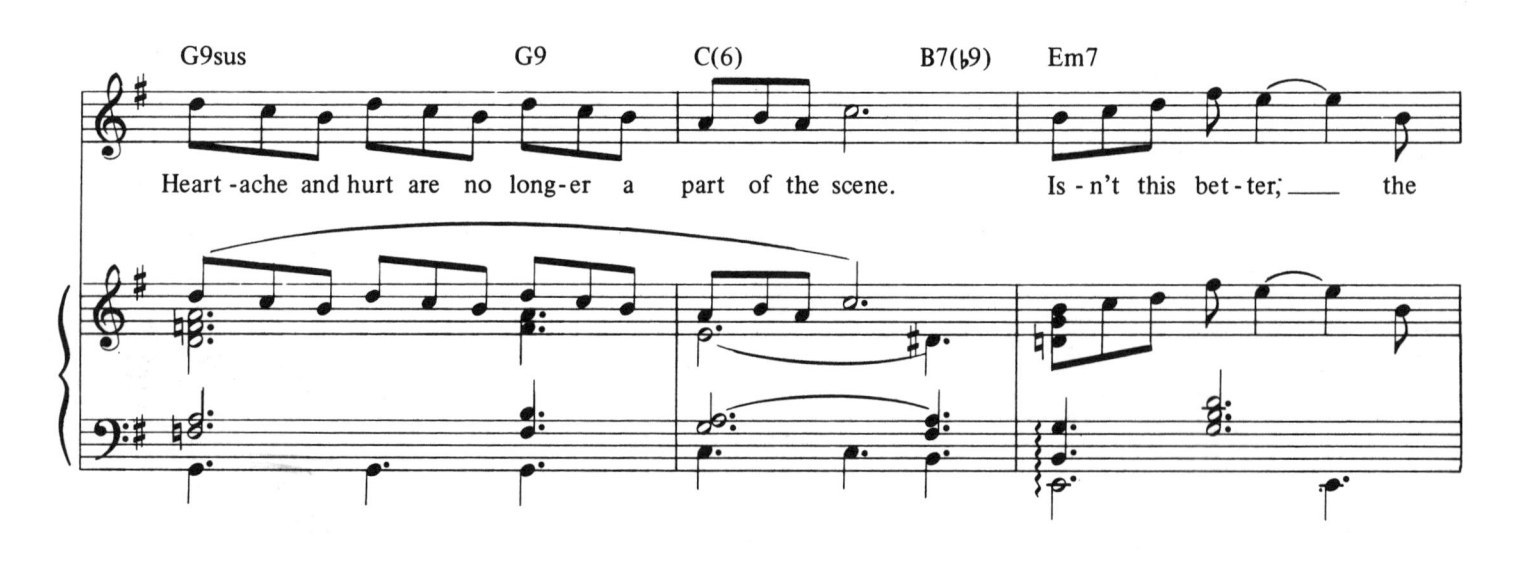

Heart - ache and hurt are no long - er a part of the scene. Is - n't this bet - ter; _____ the

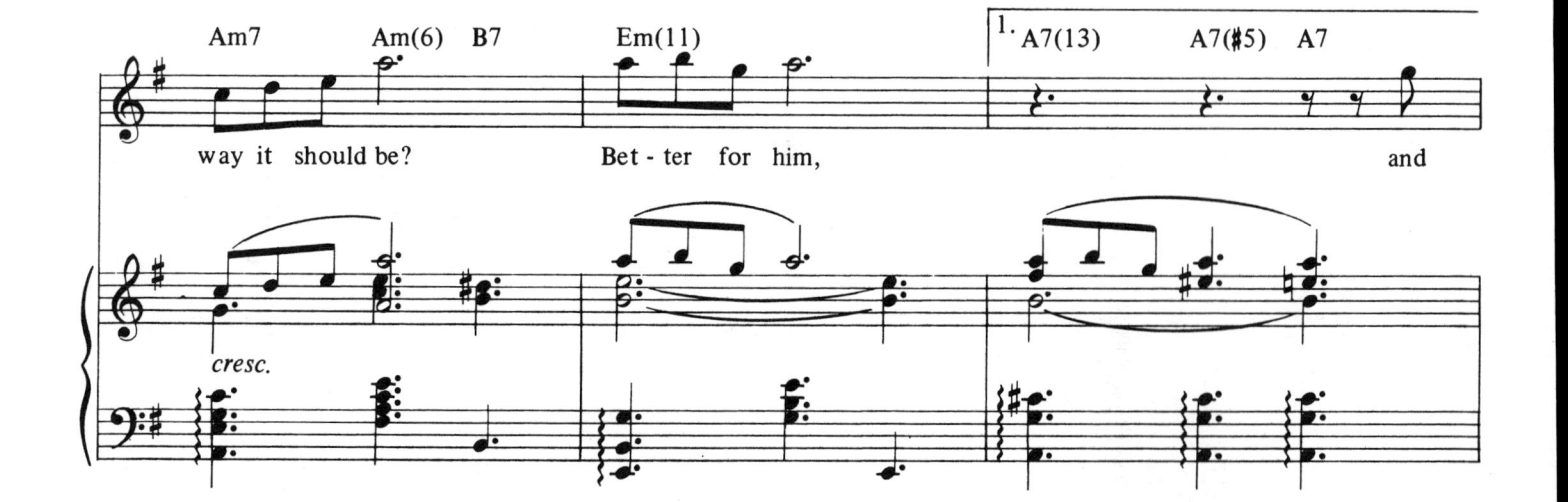

way it should be? Bet - ter for him, and

MONEY, MONEY

Lyrics by FRED EBB
Music by JOHN KANDER

world go a-round. Of that we both are sure. *(Raspberry)* on be-ing

poor. Mon-ey, mon-ey, mon-ey, mon-ey, mon-ey, mon-ey, mon-ey, mon-ey, mon-ey, mon-ey, mon-ey, mon-ey,

mon. When you have-n't an-y coal in the stove and you freeze in the win-ter and you curse to the wind at your

curse to the wind at your fate. When you haven't an-y shoes on your feet and your coat's thin as pa-per and you

fate. When you haven't an-y shoes on your feet and your coat's thin as pa-per and you look thir-ty pounds un-der-

151

CABARET

Lyrics by FRED EBB
Music by JOHN KANDER

154

NEW YORK, NEW YORK

Lyrics by FRED EBB
Music by JOHN KANDER

Moderately, with rhythm

Start spread-in' the news, I'm leav-ing to-day, I wan-na be a part____ of it New York, New